ENCOURAGEMENT FOR THE BODY OF CHRIST

Embrace & Activate the Key

Minister Vanessa Jackson

Unless otherwise indicated, all Scripture quotations are taken from the *King James Version* of the Bible.

ENCOURAGEMENT FOR THE BODY OF CHRIST

Copyright 2016 by Vanessa Jackson
Women of Faith Prayer Ministries
P.O. Box 642
Park Forest, IL 60466

ISBN: 978-0-9971579-6-3

Library of Congress Control Number: 2016910021

Printed in the United States of America All rights reserved under International Copyright Law. Contents and/or cover may not be reproduced in whole or in part in any form without the express written consent of the Author and/or Publisher.

DEDICATION

To the Body of Christ!

I dedicate this book to the entire Body of Christ. The purpose of writing this book is to encourage the Body of Christ as it faces turbulent and challenging times in both the natural and spiritual realm. For various reasons, Christians have a tendency to keep life's issues bottled up inside, sharing very little, if any, of the pain they feel with those closest to them. On the other hand, some people share too much information, resulting in heartbreak and disappointment. This book is intended to encourage Christians to lean closely and solely on the word of God, which is a sure foundation for the Body of Christ.

Whatever test or trial we face, we must know, without a shadow of a doubt that God is with us. We can't allow life's trials to remove us from the Word of God or push us out of the Will of God. By all means, we definitely cannot let circumstances keep us from praying and having faith in what we pray about.

We must bear in mind that we have a Savior that has walked this earth, been tempted and tried, therefore, He understands first-hand what we experience and the issues we face now and in the future. We have His assurance that we are not walking alone; He is with us to lead, guide, instruct and give clarity for our lives as long as we stay with Him.

Stay Encouraged!

TABLE OF CONTENTS

Foreword 7
Origin 9
Introduction 11
Chapter 1 13
Waiting on the Lord 13
Chapter 2 18
Elevation: Fervently Seeking the Lord 18
Chapter 3 25
Don't Let Your Emotions Drive 25
Chapter 4 28
Shake It Off 28
Chapter 5 38
You Are Not Exempt 38
Chapter 6 43
Another Dip 43
Chapter 7 48
I Miss You Lord 48
Chapter 8 52
Worthy of All the Glory 52
Contact 55
What Pastors Are Saying About
"Encouragement for the Body of Christ" 57

Foreword

Jesus' disciples were asked a question from the Pharisees after they saw Jesus sit down to eat with some publicans and sinners. The question was: *"Why eateth your Master with publicans and sinners?"* Our Lord (Yeshua) heard them and he said to them, *"They that be whole need not a Physician, but they that are sick."* Matthew 9:12a.

Minister Vanessa Jackson has reached out in this most timely book to share some pertinent revelatory information from the Word of God to encourage you on your journey with the Lord.

We know that Jesus came to destroy the works of the devil. We also know that Satan is the "prince of the air." His influence on the Body of Christ has caused countless to lose hope in the Savior.

You will find while reading her book that each chapter will captivate your spirit and you will not want to put it down.

The phrases *"Shake It Off"* and *"Fight For It"* (whatever is in your way) will resonate in your spirit! Your spirit will stand up even as the dry bones in the valley did and God will blow His spirit on you. You will be encouraged and enriched to come alive again to share your testimony.

Dr. Carolyn D. Henton
Founder, Tree of Life Agape Ministries

Origin

The Lord called Vanessa Jackson to the ministry as an anointed Teacher and Prophetess. In doing so, He gave her these two scriptures: St. John 15:16 and Jeremiah 1:5 as the foundation of His call upon her life. She was licensed and ordained as a Minister of the Gospel by and under the leadership of Apostle Richard D. Henton.

Minister Vanessa Jackson is the Founder of Women of Faith Prayer Ministries, which began as a prayer line in 2000, with a few women praying via 3-way calling on their individual telephones. Over the years the prayer line has grown to include women from other cities and states calling to experience the power of prayer.

Through the guidance of the Holy Ghost, Minister Vanessa was inspired to change the prayer line to a prayer ministry, now nationally known as *Women of Faith Prayer Ministries.* The ministry's motto is *"We*

Believe in the Power of Prayer! "Minister Vanessa does not take lightly the mantle of intercessory prayer and the training of other intercessors God has given her, as she firmly believes in the power of prayer to change lives and circumstances.

On June 9, 2008, under the guidance and direction of the Holy Spirit, the ministry began having a live conference prayer line which allowed a larger number of women & men to call in at one time.

Minister Vanessa Jackson was led by the Spirit of the Lord to write this book to encourage the body of Christ. She believes that it will be a blessing to all who read it.

Introduction

As we go through our Christian walk we encounter diverse situations that only seeking the Lord will help us through once we acknowledge that Jesus Christ is the only answer and person that we can turn to and depend on. We must have a made up mind to let God handle the situation for us and not get in His way, making things worse. I wrote this book to encourage the Body of Christ through different areas of their spiritual walk. During our Christian walk, we often encounter things that are unbearable, or we feel all alone. But God is there all the time - we just have to turn to Him and ask for help. I want to encourage the Body of Christ, no matter what age you are, that you can make it with God's help, leadership and guidance. The Word of God is a sure foundation that you can stand and depend on.

Chapter 1
Waiting on the Lord

What should we do while waiting on answers or waiting for God to work it out? What should we do when waiting on a word from the Lord? What should we do when waiting on an open door? What should we do while waiting on things to turn around in your life? What should we do when we've prayed fervently and effectively and still nothing has changed? What should we do when doubt creeps in the heart and mind? What should we do when the thoughts come saying, *"How long?"* and *"When will it be my turn?"*

It is said that there are a couple of ways to deal with waiting. You can be passive in waiting. The word passive means to take no action, lacking in energy and will. The other alternative is to wait with expectancy. Expectancy means you are waiting, expecting something to happen; you are in anticipation, suspense and hope.

Isaiah 40:31 reads, *"But they that wait upon the* LORD *shall renew their strength; they shall mount up with wings as eagles; they shall run, and not be weary; and they shall walk, and not faint."*

You may say, "That is easier said than done" while in the middle of your wait. Nevertheless, we have to be steadfast and unmovable in the Word of the Lord. We have to stand on his Word because heaven and earth shall pass away but his Word will not. If He said it then it shall come to pass. The Lord's "shall's" in His word are fully loaded, but you must have and exercise faith that it shall come to pass.

During the period of waiting on answers from the Lord, we first have to examine ourselves to make sure there is no blockage which will hold up our breakthrough and blessings. Ask yourself, "Is there any unrepented sin in my life?" It is always good to keep a repenting heart in the event you are unaware of an offense made to someone by word or deed. We have to make sure to clear the runway to Heaven so that our prayers will reach beyond the ceiling. John 15:7 reads: *"If ye abide in me, and my words abide in you, ye shall ask what ye will, and it shall be done unto you."*

God's timing is not our timing. Jeremiah 29:11of the Amplified Bible reads*: "For I know the thoughts and plans that I have for you, says the Lord, thoughts and plans for welfare and peace and not for evil, to give you hope in your final outcome."*

We can stand on that hope in the Lord that He will come to our rescue and meet every need that you have before Him, and the prayer petition that you are waiting on Him to answer.

While waiting on answers, it is a good time to seek the Lord even more. We can find ourselves in prayer and consecration before the Lord. We can prepare our souls for greater things and places in the Lord. While seeking Him more we should become so inundated with and focused on the things of the Lord that we forget we are waiting for answers. In other words, lose yourself in his Word, in His presence, and in His unconditional love. We get strength when we get closer to the Lord, and our spiritual lives begin to grow even more. This becomes a testimony for us and others, and we can boldly say, *"While I was in the wait God did something for my soul. He strengthened and kept me; He opened up more understanding of who He is and what He stands for. I can see God in a new and different light because of the hunger and thirst after righteousness while waiting."*

We must recognize that God is still in control, and He has not forgotten about us. Habakkuk 1:5 reads, *"Behold ye among the heathen, and regard, and wonder marvelously; for I will work a work in your days, which ye will not believe though it be told you."*

We have to put all of our trust in the Lord. His timing is not our timing. He knows what is best for us and when to give, reveal, and manifest unto us what He has for us. Some things we are waiting on the Lord to do may very well not be His directive will for our lives. The Lord knows each and every one of our futures. He knows what is up the road on our journey. Therefore, we must be secure in the knowledge of our Lord and Savior Jesus Christ that He will not withhold any good thing from us, and will not give us something or someone that would bring harm to us.

Chapter 2
Elevation: Fervently Seeking the Lord

Matthew 6:33 reads: *"But seek ye first the kingdom of God, and his righteousness; and all these things shall be added unto you."*

Psalms 75:6 reads: *"For promotion cometh neither from the east, nor from the west, nor from the south."*

Daniel 2:21-23 reads: *"And he changeth the times and the seasons: he removeth kings, and setteth up kings: he giveth wisdom unto the wise, and knowledge to them that know understanding: He revealeth the deep and secret things: he knoweth what is in the darkness, and the light dwelleth with him. I thank thee, and praise thee, O thou God of my fathers, who hast given me wisdom and might, and hast made known unto me now what we desired of thee: for thou hast now made known unto us the king's matter.*

The Lord wants us to go to another level in Him as we seek Him. Each of us has a call on our lives. We are all called to be a witness for the Lord. To be our maximum for God we have to be prepared and have the goods. The goods are His anointing and power dwelling in our lives. Recess and lunch have been over for a long time; dinner is over and it's time to do the work of the Lord. No more excuses, detouring or procrastination. We don't want to be caught with our work undone. God himself is backing us up.

In Acts 18:9-10, this is what God told Paul: *"Then spake the Lord to Paul in the night by a vision, be not afraid, but speak, and hold not thy peace. For I am with thee, and no man shall set on thee to hurt thee: for I have much people in this city."*

We can't be afraid to open up our mouth and speak what the Lord gives us to speak, in season and out of season. I am not saying that everyone is to be a preacher or a pastor. Some are called to be evangelists, some are called to preach, to teach, to prophesy - just do the mission of the Lord. We have to stand up and be a witness at home, at work and in our communities.

When we begin to go deeper in seeking the Lord that's when elevation takes place. You may pray lying prostrate before the Lord or pray while walking - however you pray -get through to God! You will be amazed at how the Lord will begin to reveal things and show you visions and spiritual dreams with meaning. You will begin to read the word of the Lord differently, scriptures that you have read before will suddenly have a greater meaning and understanding to you and you will get a revelation of what you read. Your prayers will go into a deeper depth and the Lord will give you new tongues that you haven't spoken before.

It won't take you an hour before you finally "feel the spirit of the Lord" in prayer. You will feel his anointing and power come upon you right away; it won't be a fight nor a struggle to enter into his presence. The Lord wants to take the struggle and fight away.

The Lord wants to prepare us and instill in us everything that we need for the journey, and He wants to completely deliver us from self, other people and the deep things that we hold within that no one but the Lord knows about. He wants to take fear away. God hasn't given us the spirit of fear but of love, power and a sound mind. He wants to give us more power to do His will, but we have to be in position to receive from God. We have to be in a spiritual mind and a spiritual realm to receive and to see it - not with natural eyes but with spiritual eyes. As we get into the spiritual realm, He will begin to show us more and the things that we need in this day and hour. Even as the enemy is coming on stronger and stronger, we have to come up even the more to fight spiritually.

Some have questions regarding the call upon their lives, and the assignment the Lord has for them. As you go deeper in God, He will reveal all that you are searching for regarding your purpose in this life. Jeremiah 29:13 says, *"And ye shall seek me, and find me, when ye shall search for me with all your heart."* Also, Matthew 7:7-8 reads,

"Ask, and it shall be given you; seek, and ye shall find; knock, and it shall be opened unto you: For every one that asketh receiveth; and he that seeketh findeth; and to him that knocketh it shall be opened."

I know this is easier said than done, but we have to forget about ourselves, circumstances around us, and concentrate on Him. For we know in his Word that we should not take thought for tomorrow. Worrying is a sin, and if you think about it, what does worrying do for us? Nothing positive, but deteriorates and negatively affects our minds and bodies. Once we reach another level we will have the ability to send forth Judah, which means praise, on a higher level. Praises will rise up as you're cooking, cleaning, and even at work, and you won't behave unseemly in the workplace. You will get praise down in your spirit, and feel the need to release it. The Lord loves true praises; He inhabits the praises of men. He dwells in the praises - that is His address. While you are giving Him true praises, it will cause Him to send His angels to your rescue.

During this time of elevation, you are restored, your joy which is strength, is full, you are more determined, encouraged, boldness for the Lord is heightened, and your smile will return. Those around you will see a difference in you, there will be a glow on your countenance which is the glory of the Lord as a result of spending quality time with Him in prayer.

This is not the time to put on brakes but to drive and go forward in prayer like never before! We are in the end time and this is when we will see who is strong enough to endure to the end… even in the midst of heated times. Every sin has come on strong and bold in the world and as saints we can't stay seated but we must rise to the occasion, which is the word of the Lord. We are not to waiver in our faith or in our prayers; we are to pray without ceasing.

That doesn't mean you have to always be on your knees, or screaming to the top of your lungs, but you can whisper a prayer at work, in the car or on public transportation, in the store, wherever you are the Lord will hear you. Also, ask the Lord to cover your prayer with the Blood of Jesus so that hindrance and retaliation do not come from the devil, but will ward him off at the door. Remember you really can get a breakthrough when you pray for others and travail in the spirit for their troubles and circumstances. You are then exercising unselfish love through intercessory prayer for your brothers and sisters in Christ. That doesn't mean you have to stop praying for yourself, just spread your prayers around and don't forget to pray for your enemies.

We want to get deeply rooted in prayer so that we can have prayers stored up for those stormy days in our lives and the lives of others.

Chapter 3
Don't Let Your Emotions Drive

Emotions are a natural instinctive state of mind deriving from one's circumstances, moods, or relationships with others.

Proverbs 3:5-6
"Trust in the LORD with all thine heart; and lean not unto thine own understanding. In all thy ways acknowledge him, and he shall direct thy paths."

*The key word here is **trust.**

Trust is defined as a firm belief in the reliability, truth, and ability, or strength of someone or something. It also means having confidence, belief, and faith. We know that *"without faith it is impossible to please him,"* according to Hebrews 11:6. Faith is having an assurance.

Here are some of the emotions that we may encounter, potentially creating hindrance.

Affection, Anger, Anguish, Annoyance, Anxiety, Apathy, Awe, Boredom, Confidence, Contempt, Courage, Curiosity, Depression, Desire, Despair, Disappointment, Disgust, Distrust, Dread, Ecstasy, Embarrassment, Envy, Excitement, Fear, Frustration, Gratitude, Grief, Guilt, Happiness, Hatred, Hope, Hostility, Horror, Hurt, Interest, Joy, Jealousy, Loneliness, Love, Outrage, Panic, Passion, Pity, Regret, Remorse, Relief, Sadness, Satisfaction, Self Confidence, Shame, Shock, Shyness, Suffering, Surprise, Terror, Trust, Wonder, Worry, Zeal and Zest.

Emotions are often associated and considered influential with mood, temperament, personality, disposition, and motivation, as well as influenced by hormones. Emotions are often the driving force behind motivation, whether positive or negative.

It is good to have open communication with the Lord, telling Him all that is bothering you and exactly how you feel. Although He already knows what is going on inside of us,

He wants us to feel comfortable in confessing it to Him. During open communication with the Lord, you can ask Him how to exercise control over your emotions. Jesus gives us the tools and knowledge to manage our emotions and not let emotions govern our lives. We can use the weapon of pleading the blood of Jesus over our thoughts when the enemy paints negative pictures, brings doubt, fear, and rejection.

Some may feel more comfortable talking with someone whom they can trust and confide in. Vent in a healthy way to release frustrations, which lifts a great load off of you. Take control and do not let your emotions do the driving, which often causes a wreck in your life.

Chapter 4
Shake It Off

Whatever the devil is trying to put on you, SHAKE IT OFF! We have to exercise authority over the enemy!

Acts 28:3-6 states, *"And Paul had gathered a bundle of sticks, and laid them on the fire, there came a viper out of the heat, and fastened on his hand. Before this incident the devil tried to kill Paul in a storm but of course he failed, so he is now trying again. The devil will just keep trying over and over to break you down and take you out. But we can't let him. And when the barbarians saw the venomous beast hang on his hand, they said among themselves, No doubt this man is a murderer, whom though he hath escaped the sea, yet vengeance suffereth not to live. The Barbarians knew that this type of viper would kill any man. A little note the Barbarians where people of a different language and culture and usually they lived outside the Roman Empire. And he shook* *off the beast into the fire, and felt no harm. Now when Paul shook the viper off that didn't mean he didn't feel the pain of the bite. When we go through our personal trials and tribulations, something's hurt and is painful. We have to shake if off of us and don't dwell in the pain and hurt. Howbeit they looked when he should have swollen, or fallen down dead suddenly: but after they had looked a great while, and saw no harm come to him, they changed their minds, and said that he was a god."*

God's covering and protection was with Paul. We have the blood of Jesus covering us as well.

Isaiah 54:17 reminds us that, *"No weapon that is formed against thee shall prosper; and every tongue that shall rise against thee in judgment thou shalt condemn. This is the heritage of the servants of the LORD, and their righteousness is of me, saith the LORD."*

The Word of God doesn't say that the weapon wouldn't be formed, but it does assure us that it shall not prosper. Whatever the enemy has planned you have to know that God said that it will not prosper. Speak in authority with belief and faith in what God said…**NO WEAPON!**

1 Peter 5:8
"Be sober, be vigilant; because your adversary the devil [the devil is always on his job], as a roaring lion, walketh about, seeking whom he may devour:"

The word sober means to have self-control. The word vigilant means to be awake & watchful. We must be watchful & prayerful at all times because Satan is ready to attack at any given moment. Although the enemy is always on his job, we must have our spiritual dukes up and the full armor of the Lord on at all times.

Luke 10:19
"Behold, I give unto you power to tread on serpents and scorpions, and over all the power of the enemy: and nothing shall by any means hurt you."

We have spiritual authority over the enemy. That is how Paul was able to walk away from the viper bite as he shook it off. Don't accept what the enemy offers you. It maybe something that you were delivered from and he's trying to bind you with it again, but SHAKE IT OFF!

As a born again believer we have the power to shake it off! As we have already read in Luke, the Lord gives us power. If you are up against peer pressure (this is not limited to teenagers or young adults, but everyone can experience peer pressure.) Perhaps you were delivered from drugs, premarital sex, promiscuity, alcoholism, etc.; whatever it may be, and the enemy is trying to get you to go back to that lifestyle – SHAKE IT OFF! DON'T ACCEPT IT!!

Some of the ways to "shake it off" are prayer, fasting, praising and worshipping the Lord, reading the word of God, staying connected with God, and staying close to the fire and anointing.

Shake off depression, sadness, and anger. We can't let the cares of this world bring us down and all that is going on in our generation. People are simply angry with everyone, and may want to approach you in a negative manner or may even accuse you falsely. SHAKE IT OFF!

People come from various backgrounds, personalities, and carry different spirits. As a result, they exhibit conflicting behavior. As you interact with them, it appears that everything is fine. Suddenly, you see a different side, and without warning, you're attacked.

The enemy doesn't care who or what he uses. We see him at work in the world around us, with the senseless killings and the passing of ungodly laws. Sin is raging rampantly in television programs. Society says that certain behavior is acceptable and okay, even if it is contrary to God's word. We have to shake off what the world is trying to entangle us with. It is another tactic of the enemy, but he is yet a liar! God is still in control. He is still King of Kings and Lord of Lords. He is our Shepherd and we shall not want for anything.

Shake off the temptations of this world. As stated in Ephesians 6:11, *"Put on the whole armour of God that ye may be able to stand against the wiles of the devil.* James 4:7 also tells us to *"Submit yourselves therefore to God. Resist the devil, and he will flee."* This Scripture suggests that we can't be weak. It is imperative that we remain strong to survive.

It is evident that we are in spiritual warfare – a warfare that has to be fought in the spirit, and not in the natural.

God is able to keep you from falling. Jude1:24 put it this way: *"Now unto him that is able to keep you from falling, and to present you faultless before the presence of his glory with exceeding joy."*

Make every effort to avoid areas of weakness which may cause you to fall, which include situations, places, people, and things. You can be a leader in the concept of "Shaking It Off." You can be an encouragement to your friends, family and other circles of influence in which you come in contact with on a regular basis. If they are saved, they too have the power to shake it off.

Shake off the spirit of suicide!
Shake off the "I don't care" spirit!
Shake off sickness!
Shake off poverty!
Shake off the mind to backslide!
Shake off the spirit of unforgiveness!
Shake off pity parties!
Shake off the mind and urge to get drunk or high!

SHAKE IT OFF!

Yes, this is a spiritual fight. If you are in the Army of the Lord, you have to fight. There are no ifs, ands or buts about it; you have to put up your spiritual dukes and fight!
Fight for your salvation!
Fight for your right mind!
Fight for your health!
Fight for your children!

Fight for your spouses!
Fight for your financial stability!
Fight to keep your praise!
Fight to keep your dance!
Fight for the victory!
Fight for peace and serenity in your life!
Fight for a consistent prayer life!

We have to fight the good fight of Faith. As we stay in the fight spiritually, at any age, our spiritual muscles are developed and strengthened. The spiritual muscles get stronger, so when things, issues, or temptations come our way, we have the strength to Shake It Off!

We have the power to bind up things that the enemy throws our way, and to loose things off of us. Matthew 16:19 says, *"And I will give unto thee the keys of the kingdom of heaven: and whatsoever thou shalt bind on earth shall be bound in heaven: and whatsoever thou shalt loose on earth shall be loosed in heaven."*

Again, the Lord tells us that we have power in addition to Him backing us up in Heaven!

This power is nothing we get or did on our own. We are nothing without the Lord and can't do anything without Him.

He gives us the tools that we need to make it and get the job done. All we have to do is utilize them. Don't sit on them or set them aside to get rusty. We cannot operate in this power if we are fearful. He did not give us the spirit of fear but of love and power and a sound mind.

We have to continue to exercise our faith. As my late Apostle preached, *"My Faith Tells Me All Is Well."* Go with that, walk in it, talk it and dwell in the fact that "all is well" with you.

We are going to shake some things off of us; we don't need extra baggage or garbage. We are going to shake ourselves free!

Additionally, don't be a garbage can, meaning don't let people infiltrate your spirit, dumping negativity, gossip, and nasty attitudes into you. We are to keep our temples clean, because the Holy Ghost does not dwell in an unclean temple.

Some may need to shake off bad relationships or so-called friends. Unfortunately, we can't be close friends with everybody, but we can pray for them and love them from a distance. Surround yourself with people who are strong and are striving to grow and go higher in the Lord. They will help you through the rough places in your life. You cannot keep company with people who are judgmental and bringing you down all the time.

Tell yourself that you are a new person, walk with your head up, not stuck up, but encouraged in this Christian war and walk. You have to loose yourself from bondage, for whom the son makes free will be free indeed.

Chapter 5
You Are Not Exempt

Encouragement for our Youth

Philippians 2:10-11 says, *"That at the name of Jesus every knee should bow of things under the earth. And that every tongue should confess that Jesus Christ is Lord, to the glory of God the father."*

Joel 2:28 reads, *"And it shall come to pass afterward, that I will pour out my spirit upon all flesh; and your sons and daughters shall prophesy, your old men shall dream dreams, your young men shall see visions."*

Some may think that God wasn't speaking to us because this scripture is from the Old Testament, but this scripture is also reiterated in the New Testament, in Acts 2:17: *"And it shall come to pass in the last day saith God, I will pour out my spirit upon all flesh; and your sons and daughters shall prophesy, and your young men shall see visions, and your old men shall dream dreams."*

Everyone on this earth has to answer to God one day, whether young, middle-aged or old, as stated in Romans 14:11: *"For it is written, As I live, saith the Lord, every knee shall bow to me, and every tongue shall confess to God."*

If you are thinking, *"I am young. I can wait until I am older because this church stuff is for older people. I have to do my own thing.* "You are wrong because every day a young person's life is taken from him or her and if they didn't know the Lord Jesus Christ they will spend eternity in hell. Or you might say, *"I will repent (ask for forgiveness) on my death bed.* "Who's to say if you will be in a coma and never wake up to repent. We can't use the excuse that I can't live a saved life because the church is too strict or boring. God can help each of us in our walk with Him. He is our strength and is able to help you live a Godly life. You have to pray and ask the Lord to give you the strength to stand for him. If you can't stand for Him you will fall for anything. Some may say, *"I am not a bad person, I don't do drugs; I don't party all night; I don't drink; I don't sleep around. I go to church every Sunday."* But did you know that the devil goes to church faithfully every Sunday too, and on other church days as well? So, what is your excuse for not confessing your sins and coming whole-heartedly on the Lord's side? You can't straddle the fence - you are either going to be in or out.

Jesus speaks in Revelation 3:15-16, saying, *"I know thy works, that thou art neither cold nor hot: I would thou wert cold or hot. So then because thou art lukewarm, and neither cold nor hot, I will spue thee out of my mouth."*

God is a deliverer for whatever you may be going through that you haven't shared with anyone. He's the best friend you will ever have. He is someone you can talk to anytime of the day and He won't share with others what you share with him. He won't tell anyone or gossip behind your back. His grace and mercy is sufficient enough for you and me.

There is a song that says, *"Come on in this house, it's going to rain, rain down fire it's going to rain. You'd better come on in this house it's going to rain. Door stands wide open just call his name, don't wait too late because it's going to rain. Come on follow me it's going to rain, you don't need no ticket it's going to rain."*

Young people don't get caught in the rain. I say to everyone, don't wait too late because you are not exempt. To those that are saved and living a clean life, stay encouraged and don't get weary in well doing. Don't allow your peers to sway you away from the Lord. I know there are many temptations out there to get your attention, but if you plan on making it in this world and to Heaven, you must continue to fight the good fight of faith in the Lord.

I Timothy 6:12 says, *"Fight the good fight of faith, lay hold on eternal life, whereunto thou art also called, and hast professed a good profession before many witnesses."*

Keep your eyes on Christ and the prize.

I'd like to share a personal testimony. The Lord saved me when I was sixteen years old. I was blessed to live a saved life 2 ½ years in high school. I know from experience that God is a keeper, if you want to be kept. Through all the trials and tribulations, I still had a mind to be saved.

Chapter 6
Another Dip

Acts 2:1-4 reads, *"And when the day of Pentecost was fully come they were all with one accord in one place. And suddenly there came a sound from heaven as of a rushing mighty wind, and it filled all the house where they were sitting. And there appeared unto them cloven tongues like as of fire, and it sat upon each of them. And they were all filled with the Holy Ghost, and began to speak with other tongues, as the Spirit gave them utterance.* After *the Holy Ghost fell others were looking on and were mocking them like what's wrong with them they must be drunk with that new wine."*

Acts 2:14-21 reads, Acts 2:14-21 reads, *"But Peter, standing up with the eleven, lifted up his voice, and said unto them, Ye men of Judaea, and all ye that dwell at Jerusalem, be this known unto you, and hearken to my words: For these are not drunken, as ye suppose, seeing it is* but *the third hour of the day. But this is that which was spoken by the prophet Joel; And it shall come to pass in the last days, saith God, I will pour out of my Spirit upon all flesh: and your sons and your daughters shall prophesy, and your young men shall see visions, and your old men shall dream dreams: And on my servants and on my handmaidens I will pour out in those days of my Spirit; and they shall prophesy: And I will shew wonders in heaven above, and signs in the earth beneath; blood, and fire, and vapour of smoke: The sun shall be turned into darkness, and the moon into blood, before that great and notable day of the Lord come: And it shall come to pass,* that *whosoever shall call on the name of the Lord shall be saved."*

We all need another dip. There is one baptism but there are many refilling's. We need to have the Holy Ghost in depth. We want or *should* want the fire as described in verse 3: *"the cloven tongues like fire strong cutting tongues.* "It's the fire that you feel down in your belly and in your hands. Jesus was full of the Holy Ghost. Luke 4:1 says,

"And Jesus being full of the Holy Ghost returned from Jordan, and was led by the Spirit into the wilderness." This should be our desire. Isaiah 11:2 reads, *"And the spirit of the Lord shall rest upon him, the spirit of wisdom and understanding, the spirit of counsel and might, the spirit of knowledge and the fear of the Lord."*

We need more power because for every level there is another devil, which means we have to be equipped to do the work of the Lord. If we go back a little in the scriptures, Acts 1:8 reads, *"But ye shall receive power after that the Holy Ghost is come upon you and ye shall be witnesses unto me both Jerusalem, and in all Judaea and Samaria, and unto the uttermost part of the earth."*

There is something great and miraculous happening. God's power will be demonstrated even more in this time in which we live. We have to prepare ourselves for the move of God upon His people and upon this generation. We need another dip because even as the devil is coming on stronger in our world today, we have to be able to fight in the spirit realm again the attack of the enemy. We can't be weak soldiers in the Lord's army. We need to be as close to the Lord as possible in these last and evil days. Even as the word of God is being fulfilled, that which He already warned us that was going to happen is certainly being manifested.

In getting another dip, we will be more stronger in our faith to believe God when we pray for other's that are bound and those that don't know the Lord. We will have more power to bind and loose in the name of Jesus. Please don't think that you don't need another dip if you are of the fivefold ministry. We all need more of the Lord to be our maximum for him. We should desire to be baptized even the more with his anointing, for it is the anointing that breaks the yokes. Whatever we do for the Lord we want it to count, we should want it to be affective. We should desire the wisdom of the Lord to go forth in his name, whether it is witnessing or preaching or counseling and praying for people.

Another dip not satisfied where you are but desiring more of him in and around your life and your every being.

Chapter 7
I Miss You Lord

Matthew 5:6 says, *"Blessed are they which do hunger and thirst after righteousness for they shall be filled."*

Luke 6:21 says, *"Blessed are you who hunger now, for you shall be filled. Blessed are ye that weep now: for ye shall laugh."*

In Psalms 51:10-12, David asks God to create within Him a clean heart and renew a right spirit within him; to cast him not away from the Lord's presence and take not the Holy Spirit from him. He also asks God to restore unto him the joy of God's salvation and uphold him with His free spirit.

If we really desire change and want the Lord to dwell in us, we have to get desperate. In other words, we have to pray more, fast more, read the Word more and ready to hear a word from the Lord at any given time. We want to get to a place where we are prayed up. There may come a time in your life when you're not able to pray, but if you have prayers stored up, they will bring you through.

I am talking about reaching a place in God that will blow your mind, and will fill voids in your life, in your heart, in your spirit, and in your belly. These are spiritual voids that can only be filled by God Himself –not by man or by material things. This is a thirst for God's presence that natural water cannot quench. I am talking about the peace of God all over you, knowing that He hears your cry and fervent prayer. This is your personal SOS. The desperation that makes you cry for no apparent reason. The kind of desperation that makes you cry out and tell the Lord, *"Lord I miss you. I miss your presence. I miss your anointing. I miss your power. I miss the comfort of knowing I am in your directive will. I miss your voice speaking to me. I miss the comfort of your arms around me. I miss you Lord."*

Desperation for God requires seeking a quiet place where you can hear a Rhema word from the Lord. You reach a point where nothing or no one else can help you but God. In the midst of truly seeking God, you will find joy because the joy of the Lord is your strength, according to Nehemiah 8:10.

We find ourselves praying to the Lord do not pass me by. Sometimes we question whether or not God hears our prayers. I am here to let you know that God does hear us. Psalms 66:19 states, *"But verily God hath heard me; he hath attended to the voice of my prayer."*

As God begins to strengthen you, you find tears streaming down your face. You feel chills of His awesome presence all over. You feel the warmth of his anointing in your belly and in your hands. You will get a witness down in your sanctified soul that God has heard your cry and is there to fill the void.

You will feel different in your spirit and praise from deep within your belly and soul comes forth for the lover of your soul. God loves it when we give Him praise and cry out to Him in gratitude, and sincerely long to be closer to Him. He begins to open our spiritual ears and eyes, so that we can hear and see what he is saying to us and showing us in the spirit. We get the revelation and understanding of why He took us that way. We thank Him for the strength and ability to acknowledge that we have a void in our lives, and the desire for more of Him. I believe that when God puts a greater yearning in our spirits for the more of Him, he has something planned for our lives and wants us to be in the right place to receive it. We have to continue to reach out and go after what God has for us. What God has for you is for you.

Chapter 8
Worthy of All the Glory

Psalms 19:1
"God is worthy of worship because he is in everything He created. God created the heaven and the earth. He is worthy of worship simply because everything is His. All of creation - from the skies, to the trees, to the people - were carefully crafted by His hands for a purpose. All things were made to glorify the Creator. God is worthy of worship because His law is consistent with His perfect and true nature."

God knows what is best for us, and His way is perfect, sure, wise, joyful, pure, revealing, clean, enduring, true, righteous, valuable, sweet, and full of conviction. We worship God because His way is the only perfect and trustworthy way.

I Chronicles 16:25-29
"As we choose to give God glory we have so many reasons to celebrate daily. In our adoration, we set aside our fleshly nature to

be set apart for God. As we worship the Lord of heaven & earth, we experience the beauty of his holiness. The reasons for giving glory to God will never run out. He's been so good, so faithful, so true and so loving. He is a provider and a keeper, and He is trustworthy."

Psalm 29:1-3
"Give unto the Lord, O ye mighty, give unto the Lord glory and strength. 2. Give unto the Lord the glory due unto his name; worship the Lord in the beauty of holiness. 3. The voice of the Lord is upon the waters: the God of glory thundereth: the Lord is upon many waters."

In Psalms 96:1-13, all the earth is summons to give glory to God. When Christ completed His work on earth, He entered into His glory in heaven, clothed in the robe of majesty and crowned in glory; the beauty of holiness is characterized in Christ Jesus.

As we worship in true holiness, the real beauty of God Himself is revealed. It is the beauty of the angels giving Him glory in the heavenly realm; it is the beauty of the saints partaking of God's divine nature. The desire to give glory to God extends beyond praise and worship. If we don't cry out to the Lord, the rocks will, and we don't want rocks taking our place. Angels don't have the experience of being redeemed, set free and saved from sin. They don't have the experience of being filled with the Holy Ghost.

When things seem to be going wrong or maybe you just came through a bad situation and turn around, here comes another one, God is still worthy of all the glory!

We can command ourselves to give God the glory that He deserves.

Contact

Minister Vanessa Jackson
Email: veryblesswoman1@sbcglobal.net

Visit Vanessa Jackson on facebook

Women of Faith Prayer Ministries
P.O. Box 642
Park Forest, Illinois 60466
Prayer Line:
1-218-339-6427 passcode 7777#
Prayer Request and Comment Line:

1-641-715-3900 ext. 435144#

Connect with the

Women of Faith Prayer Ministries on

Facebook

What Pastors Are Saying About "Encouragement for the Body of Christ"

"Encouragement is defined as the persuasion to do or to continue something. During these last and evil days, it is imperative that the body of Christ continues on in the work of the Lord, being His voice in the earth. Encouragement for the Body of Christ is designed to motivate, inspire and give confidence to God's people, specifically to those who labor among the five-fold ministry gifts. If you have found yourself in a state of discouragement, disappointment or even hopelessness, this book is for you! As you read, be lifted….be persuaded …be stimulated….and be encouraged to move forward in Christ Jesus!!!"

Thanking God for His Love
Assistant Pastor J. Denise Ray
Church on the Rock
Matteson, Illinois

"All Blessings, Glory and Honor to Our King! Thank you Minister Vanessa for the opportunity to review this magnificent book given to you by Our Lord and Savior Jesus Christ! As I reviewed each page one by one, I could not help but see the need for this book in the lives of all individuals and ministries. I call it the "A through Z" book. It covers absolutely every area of our lives! As a Christian of 31+ years, a Minister of 29+ years and Pastor 5+ years, my heart, mind, body and soul were deeply touched through the depth and sincerity of this work. I decree and declare to you Minister Vanessa, you are long-lived, stable, durable, and incorruptible; full of peace, patience and love, and whatsoever you set your hands to do shall prosper, in JESUS name, Amen. And to all who is blessed to partake of this book, you are richly blessed naturally and spiritually; your life will never be the same again!"

BLESSINGS,

Bishop Phillip M. Gordon
Divine Destiny International Ministries
Little Rock, Arkansas

Minister Vanessa,

I love the origin of the book, how God called you and confirmed the call with His word. In the chapter, *"Shake It Off,"* I love the revelation of shaking the beast off. In this book I felt as if you took me on a journey of freedom and you explained every step. For example, in the chapter *"Shake It Off,"* if a reader struggled with depression you showed them how to shed it.

You showed us different levels, you showed us how to fight, and then you backed it up with the Word.

I felt like I was in prayer with you as I read this book. I was learning how to get free and live in victory. In the Elevation chapter you showed us how to be promoted and how to go to another level. You showed us how to get free and stay free by taking another dip. You showed us that it is for everybody and that no one is exempt. It is for sons and daughters and as many as the Lord shall call. On this journey you encouraged our walk with the Lord by teaching us to seek his face. And then in the last chapter, you pointed us to Him and gave Him all the glory.

Great job Minister Vanessa and may God richly bless you.

Senior Pastor Angie Hogan
Freedom Ministries Church
Crossett, Arkansas

"I really believe this book is going to help the body of Christ on how to wait & trust in God, and what he requires us to do. We as a body should be an example for living a holy life. This is a good read Woman of God. The chapter *"Don't Let Your Emotions Drive"* is a very good chapter."

Prophet Mario Caple
Vision Kingdom Learning Center
Chicago, Illinois

www.ingramcontent.com/pod-product-compliance
Lightning Source LLC
Chambersburg PA
CBHW031428040426
42444CB00006B/734